Vegan
Slow Cooker

Healthy Plant-Based Vegan
Crock Pot Recipes

Madison Miller

ISBN: 978-1986128056

Printed in the United States

Contents

Contents

Introduction

"You're vegan? What do you even eat?"

You've probably heard this question 101 times since you decided to make the ethical and sustainable choice to go vegan. Your answer is probably, "Umm… everything that doesn't come from animals?" People are usually flabbergasted by this, but the fact is that a lot of food is already vegan—and with a little creativity and the right ingredients, you can vegan-ify almost anything else.

People often think that being vegan is limiting or a diet, but that's just not the case. Most vegans love food; they just choose to make their ethics and values a priority when choosing what to eat.

If you're new to vegan cooking, you might have some questions, so before you jump into the delicious and easy recipes in this book, take some time to read the introduction for tips, tricks, and helpful information.

"Where do you get your protein?"

This is another annoying question that vegans get asked all of the time. People act like meat and dairy are the only sources of protein in the world!

The fact is that most people in developed countries actually get too much protein. If you're new to the vegan diet, you should spend some time counting protein and planning your meals to make sure you're getting enough, but rest assured that protein deficiency is relatively rare.

Amino acids are organic compounds responsible for a wide variety of processes in the body. When they bind together in long chains, they make proteins. While our bodies can produce many of their own amino acids, there are nine types which the human body cannot create on its own. This means that we rely on our food for these.

Something vegans should keep in mind is that not all sources of protein have all of the amino acids that you need. In fact, most don't. But no need to worry: As long as you are able to get all of these amino acids within one day, you should be fine.

Practically, that means that you can't rely on just one or two sources of protein a day. When you're eating vegan, a good rule of thumb is that each meal should have two kinds of protein. This may sound like trouble, but you'd be surprised how many foods contain protein. Once you get used to eating a vegan diet and creative cooking, getting enough protein is something you won't even think about.

Check with a nutritionist or online to find out how many grams of protein you should be eating in a day. To make things easier, each of the recipes in this cookbook details how many grams of protein are in a serving.

If you're sick of answering the protein question, check out these common vegan proteins, how to use them, and their nutritional benefits.

Black Beans
Did you know that the darker the color of a bean, the more antioxidants it has? Black beans are definitely a vegan staple. With 15 grams of protein per cooked cup, plus 15 grams of fiber, black beans are a great way to make a meal more filling. From

Mexican food to brownies (that's right, brownies) this cookbook has plenty of recipes that integrate this filling bean.

Walnuts
Nuts and seeds are another source of protein for vegans. Rich in healthy fats and protein, this nut is a great snack or addition to a meal to help you feel full. Add crushed walnuts to desserts, pasta, or even pizza!

Quinoa
Quinoa might just be the king of vegan protein. Once eaten by Incan warriors, this seed (yes, quinoa is technically a seed, although it's served as a grain) serves up a complete amino acid group. That means that if you eat quinoa, you won't have to worry about combining proteins. Quinoa is great in salads, made into a veggie burger, or served with curry. You can even find pasta made out of quinoa at your local health food store.

Chickpeas
This versatile legume isn't just for hummus (although hummus is a delicious vegan staple you should master). Chickpeas have 14.5 grams of protein per cooked cup, plus 11 grams of fiber, manganese, and folate, a nutrient important for women. Chickpeas are great in curries, salads, stews, and so much more.

Oats
There's no vegan breakfast quite as delicious as oatmeal loaded with cinnamon and brown sugar, and that's hardly the only good thing about oats. Oats have been proven to help reduce cholesterol, so if you went vegan for your heart health (good move) you should add oats into your diet whenever you can. Gluten-free? No worries! You can easily find gluten-free oats and oat flour.

Tofu

Made from soy beans, tofu is a vegan classic, but most non-vegans turn their nose up at it. Why has tofu gotten such a bad reputation? Who knows, but with the recipes in this book, even your carnivorous friends will become tofu enthusiasts. With just 178 calories—but 12 grams of protein—per serving, no vegan diet is complete without tofu. Bread it, fry it, bake it, or blend it; the possibilities are endless, so get creative with this protein-packed treat.

Be sure to buy GMO-free tofu, as the health effects of consuming genetically modified soybeans are unclear.

Lentils

Lentils are a legume that appears across the world, from French cuisine to Indian food, and frequently in this cookbook. With 18 grams of protein per cooked cup, lentils are a perfect addition to stews, veggie burgers, salads, and meat replacements.

"Can you eat this?"

The quick answer to this question is yes. As a vegan, you can technically eat anything; you just choose not to. Whether you chose to become vegan for health reasons, weight loss, the environment, your love of animals, or all of the above, don't let your lifestyle choice make you feel limited. With some practice and creativity, eating vegan can open new doors of culinary delights, rather than closing them.

"Is this really vegan?"

You may find yourself asking that when you're eating at a vegan restaurant. How can they make food so creamy, buttery, or cheesy without using dairy? The answer is vegan hacks. There are a few staples that every vegan should be familiar with. These staples help to emulate flavors not usually associated with a plant-based diet.

Once you've mastered these ingredients, you'll hear a chorus of "Is this really vegan?" at your next dinner party.

Cashews
No vegan pantry is complete without cashews. Soak these babies in water for a few hours, drain, and blend with herbs and spices to make creamy dipping sauces, or with sugar and cocoa powder for vegan ice cream. The high-protein possibilities are practically endless. Cashew "milk" shakes, anyone?

Nutritional Yeast
Nutritional yeast has a cheesy flavor, making it most vegans' first choice when it comes to cheese replacements. It's super-low in calories but high in protein, with just 40 calories and 3 grams of protein per tablespoon. Most vegans just can't live without nutritional yeast, and retailers know this; that's why it often comes fortified with vitamins that vegans tend to lack, like vitamin B_{12}. Why take a multivitamin if you can just eat creamy, delicious vegan queso every day?

Tahini
Like cashews and nutritional yeast, tahini is an easy way to add more protein to a meal. It's also rich in healthy fats. Tahini can bring creaminess to a recipe, as well as a nutty flavor, making it a great addition to curries and stir fries. Tahini is also a perfect

base for making salad dressings and glazes. If you have a nut allergy, you can use tahini in place of nuts in lots of recipes.

Avocado

Avocado is another way to enhance creaminess in recipes. With 13 grams of fiber and 4 grams of protein per serving, avocado is as healthy as it is tasty. Use avocado to make a killer chocolate mousse or an indulgent pasta sauce. Add an avocado to a smoothie to make it even creamier.

Flax Seeds

Flax seeds are an easy way to add protein to any meal. Flax seeds are also high in omega fatty acids, which are super-important for radiant skin. Just throw some ground flax seeds into a smoothie for an instant boost. Doctors also recommend adding omega fatty acids to your diet during the winter in conjunction with vitamin D to fight off the winter blues.

As if that weren't enough, these little seeds are also a great egg replacement. Mix a tablespoon of ground flax seeds with a tablespoon of water for an instant egg substitute that you can use in almost any recipe.

Make sure you buy ground flax seeds, because your body is unable to digest them whole.

Cauliflower

Cauliflower is a low-carb replacement for rice, potatoes, and sometimes even flour, making this one of the world's most versatile vegetables. Low in calories, but high in vitamin C, cauliflower is a nutritional win-win. When cooked and blended, cauliflower gets super creamy, making it a perfect nutrient-dense cream replacement. Add to soups and curries in place of heavy cream, or use it to make "cheese."

"Is being vegan expensive?"

Some specialty items might be more expensive, but a vegan diet does not have to be an expensive endeavor. When you go to the grocery store, what's usually more expensive, meat or vegetables?

The best way to save money on a vegan diet is by shopping at local farmers' markets and buying the produce that is in season. Buying from local farmers not only supports your community, it's also more eco-friendly because the produce does not have to be transported long distances.

Check out this guide to seasonal produce.

Fall
Pomegranate, butternut squash, apples, pears, figs, sweet potatoes, arugula, beets, peppers, broccoli, celery, eggplant, cranberries, potatoes, lettuce, mushrooms, limes, pumpkins, green beans, zucchini.

Winter
Beets, cabbage, oranges, Brussels sprouts, onions, clementines, kale, cauliflower, leeks, grapefruit, lemons, mandarin oranges, shallots, radishes, turnips, winter squash, tangerines.

Spring
Asparagus, strawberries, cherries, rhubarb, kumquats, fava beans, apricots, chard, kiwis, new potatoes, peas, spinach, spring onions.

Summer

Basil, avocados, peaches, cantaloupes, blackberries, mangoes, bell peppers, lemongrass, chard, blueberries, okra, chickpeas, melons, collard greens, grapes, cucumbers, figs, plums, raspberries, spinach, watermelons, summer squash, nectarines.

Organic produce is often more expensive than conventional, but it is better for the environment and your body because it does not contain harmful pesticides and other chemicals. That being said, it's not always necessary to eat only organic produce.

Experts have developed lists called the Clean 15 and the Dirty Dozen. The Clean 15 are the 15 fruits and veggies that have the lowest levels of pesticides and are therefore safe to eat even if they aren't organic. The Dirty Dozen are the 12 fruits and vegetables highest in chemicals. You shouldn't eat these unless you can get them organic.

The Clean 15

Corn, pineapple, cauliflower, honeydew, avocado, kiwi, onions, eggplant, cabbage, sweet peas, asparagus, papaya, mangos, cantaloupe, grapefruit.

The Dirty Dozen

Spinach, pears, strawberries, bell peppers, celery, nectarines, potatoes, cherries, apples, grapes, peaches, tomatoes.

"Is being vegan a lot of work?"

Being vegan is about as much work as you want it to be. Plenty of vegans consider their diet not just a lifestyle choice but also a hobby. Cooking vegan is fun and requires creativity, so when you see your vegan friends cooking for hours every day, it's probably because they love cooking and eating delicious, healthy meals, not because they have to.

Being a vegan can be easy and low maintenance. Plenty of the recipes in this cookbook don't even require cooking and can be made in 10 minutes or less.

With all of these delicious yet nutritious options, being a vegan is really fun. As an added bonus, vegan food is usually lower in calories, which means you get to eat seemingly decadent meals without harming your health or waistline.

When vegan food can be this healthy, but taste oh so good, why would you ever eat meat or dairy?

Slow Cooker Tips

Keep It Closed

One major mistake people make when using a slow cooker is not properly sealing the lid. Since you'll likely be cooking a meal for several hours, you want to make sure the moisture is trapped to avoid burning the food. Not sealing could also allow steam to spray out and burn your hands!

Preheat

Like your oven, your slow cooker should be preheated before you add the ingredients!

Proper Care

The ceramic dish inside your slow cooker needs to be properly cleaned each time you use it. If any food is stuck to it, soak the pot overnight. The ceramic can actually be quite delicate and prone to cracking if faced with extreme changes in temperature, so do not put it in your slow cooker straight from the refrigerator.

Don't Overfill

Keep in mind that ingredients will likely expand while cooking, which means that the food within your slow cooker can become overcrowded or even spill out.

Know Your Ingredients

Not all ingredients can stand up to long exposure to heat. Some ingredients, like honey, are even said to turn toxic when heated for a long period of time. Ingredients that cannot stand the test of time should be avoided, or added in at the end. For example, pasta will often turn mushy if cooked for too long. If you're making noodle soup or a pasta dish, add your pasta in at the end and keep an eye on it.

Grease

This one is pretty self explanatory. If you don't grease the inside of your crock pot, you'll probably have to deal with burning and sticking. Not to mention how difficult it will be to clean!

Keep It Fresh

Generally, frozen ingredients don't do well in the slow cooker. Frozen foods tend to cook much faster, without releasing flavors, which defeats the purpose of slow cooking. Frozen butternut squash in particular ends up with a terrible taste and texture.

Consider Alcohol

Alcohol is a great flavor enhancer, especially for slow cooking. Because it is capable of bonding water and fat molecules together, alcohol can bind flavors that usually wouldn't jive. Note that slow cooking will not diminish alcohol content in the same way as regular cooking, so a little goes a long way. This also means you'll only want to use wine you would be willing to drink. Please be sure to keep the higher alcohol content in mind when cooking for those with alcohol issues.

Also consider vanilla extract, which contains alcohol. This won't cook away either, so use only the highest quality vanilla extract.

Breakfast

Vegan Omelet

Protein in the morning helps keep you energized throughout the day, so a protein-packed omelet is the perfect way to begin your day. Why should vegans have to miss out?

Yields: 2 servings – Preparation Time: 10 minutes – Cooking Time: 1 hour

Nutrition facts per serving: calories 356, total fat 16 g, carbs 29 g, protein 16 g, sodium 636 mg

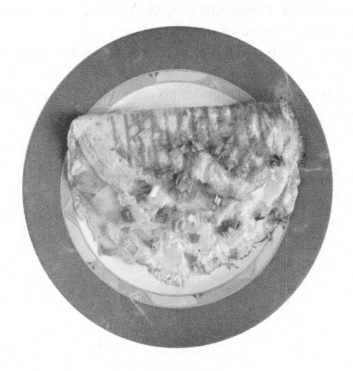

Ingredients

1 cup silken tofu
2 cloves garlic
2 tablespoons nutritional yeast
½ teaspoon turmeric
½ teaspoon paprika
½ cup mushrooms, sliced
½ bell pepper, diced
½ tomato, diced
½ cup vegan cheddar
Salt and pepper

Preparation

1. In a food processor, combine tofu, garlic, nutritional yeast, and spices. Pulse until smooth. You may need to add a tablespoon or so of water.
2. Pour mixture into the slow cooker and stir in veggies and cheese.
3. Cook covered on high for an hour or until vegetables and tofu have reached your desired tenderness.

Breakfast Casserole

Casseroles are filling meals that are easy to make. This one calls for everything but the kitchen sink, so get creative!

Yields: 4 servings – Preparation Time: 10 minutes – Cooking Time: 6 hours

Nutrition facts per serving: calories 181, total fat 8 g, carbs 25 g, protein 4 g, sodium 281 mg

Ingredients

3 cups hash brown potatoes
1 cup vegan milk
1 onion, diced
1–2 cups veggies of choice
½–1 cup vegan cheddar cheese
1 teaspoon paprika
Salt and pepper

Preparation

1. Combine all ingredients in the slow cooker. Cook covered on low for 6 hours.

Stuffed Apples

According to Ayurveda, the yogic science of nutrition, eating warm food in the morning helps get your digestion started. That makes these warm, cinnamon-y apples the perfect way to start your day.

Yields: 4 servings – Preparation Time: 10 minutes – Cooking Time: 1½ hours

Nutrition facts per serving: calories 536, total fat 22 g, carbs 78 g, protein 10 g, sodium 221 mg

Ingredients
4 apples
1 cup rolled oats
¼ cup vegan butter
5 tablespoons maple syrup
1½ teaspoons cinnamon
½ teaspoon ground ginger
¼ teaspoon ground cloves
½ cup chopped nuts

Preparation

1. Use a spoon or melon baller to scoop out the insides of the apples.
2. In a large bowl, mix together the chopped nuts, spices, butter, oats, and 2–3 tablespoons of maple syrup. Fill each apple with the mixture.
3. Place the apples in the slow cooker and cover. Cook on high until apples are soft, about 1½ hours.
4. Top with more maple syrup and a dusting of cinnamon and serve warm.

Coffee Cake

Got a sweet tooth in the morning? This cake is leagues better than eating donuts. Bring it into work to knock the socks off of your co-workers.

Yields: 6 servings – Preparation Time: 10 minutes – Cooking Time: 1½ hours

Nutrition facts per serving: calories 359, total fat 12 g, carbs 57 g, protein 6 g, sodium 88 mg

Ingredients

Cake:

1½ cups flour (oat flour if gluten-free)

½ cup maple syrup

½ cup vegan milk, unsweetened

2 tablespoons vegan butter (or coconut oil)

1 teaspoon baking soda

1 teaspoon vanilla extract

2 flax eggs

Pinch of salt

Topping:

½ cup flour

2 tablespoons brown sugar (or maple syrup)

2 tablespoons vegan butter, solid (or solid coconut oil)

1 teaspoon cinnamon

Optional:

Chopped walnuts

Preparation

1. Mix the ingredients for the topping together until crumbly; set aside.
2. Mix cake batter ingredients together. Line the slow cooker with baking paper (or better yet, slow cooker liner). Add the cake batter and layer the topping on top. Insert a paper towel beneath the lid to collect condensation.
3. Cook on high for 1½ to 2½ hours or until a toothpick comes out clean.
4. Serve warm or store for later.

Crockpot Oatmeal

Oatmeal is filling and proven to reduce cholesterol. It also has the perfect balance of protein and carbs to get your day started. This recipe will have everyone saying, "Please, sir, I want some more."

Yields: 6 servings – Preparation Time: 10 minutes – Cooking Time: 6 hours

Nutrition facts per serving: calories 523, total fat 37 g, carbs 49 g, protein 8 g, sodium 88 mg

Ingredients
4 cups vegan milk, unsweetened
1 cup steel cut oats
1–2 bananas, ripe, sliced
½ cup maple syrup
1 teaspoon cinnamon
¼ cup chopped nuts

Optional:
½ cup carob chips
1 tablespoon ground flax seeds
2 tablespoons almond butter

Preparation

1. Oil the sides of the slow cooker. Mix all ingredients (except the carob chips) in the slow cooker. Cook on low for 6–8 hours until oats are tender. Feel free to cook overnight.
2. Serve warm. Top with carob chips, maple syrup, cinnamon, or nut butter.

Breakfast Brownies

Who says brownies are for dessert? These are filled with protein and healthy fiber, guaranteed to keep you feeling full all morning.

Yields: 9 servings – Preparation Time: 10 minutes – Cooking Time: 6 hours

Nutrition facts per serving: calories 230, total fat 12 g, carbs 28 g, protein 6 g, sodium 552 mg

Ingredients
1 15-ounce can black beans, sodium free, drained and rinsed
1 cup vegan milk
½ cup oat flour
2 flax eggs
¼-½ cup cocoa powder
½ cup maple syrup
¼ cup vegan butter (or coconut oil)
2 teaspoons vanilla extract
1 teaspoon baking soda

Preparation

1. In a food processor or blender, slowly add vegan milk while blending the other ingredients together until completely smooth. You may not need to use all of the milk.
2. Cook on low for 6–8 hours until a toothpick comes out clean.

Beverages

Gingerbread Latte

There's nothing like the smell of fresh-baked gingerbread. This recipe makes a big batch, so you can share with your family during the holidays.

Yields: 8 servings – Preparation Time: 5 minutes – Cooking Time: 3 hours

Nutrition facts per serving: calories 365, total fat 36 g, carbs 12 g, protein 4 g, sodium 26 mg

Ingredients

6–8 cups coconut milk (decide based on how strong you like your lattes)
¼ cup maple syrup (or molasses)
2 teaspoons cinnamon, ground
1 teaspoon ginger, ground
½ teaspoon nutmeg, ground
½ teaspoon cloves, ground
3 cups brewed coffee
1 teaspoon vanilla extract

Optional:
⅓ cup pumpkin puree
Coconut whipped cream

Preparation

1. Combine all ingredients in the slow cooker and cook on low, covered, for 2–3 hours. Make sure it doesn't boil. You can then leave the latte on warm setting for 2 hours.
2. Serve warm topped with whipped cream and a dusting of cinnamon.

Hot Buttered Rum

Hot buttered rum is an old school way to warm up on a winter day. Surprise your friends with a vegan take on this classic.

Yields: 10 servings – Preparation Time: 5 minutes – Cooking Time: 6 hours

*Nutrition facts per serving: calories 293, total fat 9 g,
carbs 29 g, protein 0 g, sodium 105 mg*

Ingredients
2 cups brown sugar, unpacked (or maple syrup)
2 cups rum
½ cup vegan butter
2 cups water
3–5 cinnamon sticks
3–6 cloves, whole
1 teaspoon vanilla extract

Optional:
1 teaspoon orange zest
Coconut whipped cream

Preparation

1. Add all ingredients to the slow cooker. If you would like a stronger alcohol content, omit the rum at this point. Stir together, cover, and cook on low for 5–6 hours.
2. Stir in rum, if you haven't already done so, and allow to warm. Serve warm with whipped cream and a dusting of cinnamon.

Horchata Latte

Horchata is perfect for vegans because it's naturally creamy without dairy! This Latin American treat is a great addition to a pool party or beach day.

Yields: 8 servings – Preparation Time: 8 hours – Cooking Time: 4 hours

Nutrition facts per serving: calories 181, total fat 6 g, carbs 29 g, protein 2 g, sodium 6 mg

Ingredients
1 cup rice (long grain white is the most authentic Mexican option; use brown rice for a nutty flavor)
5 cups water, hot
2 tablespoons instant coffee
1 cup coconut milk
2 cinnamon sticks
⅓ cup maple syrup
1 teaspoon vanilla extract

Preparation

1. Mix the hot water, cinnamon, and rice together. Allow to sit overnight or for at least 6 hours.
2. Pour the water-and-rice mixture into the blender and blend until smooth. No need to remove the cinnamon. Strain through a cheesecloth into the slow cooker.
3. Add the maple syrup, coffee, and vanilla. Cook on low for 4 hours.
4. Serve warm, or over ice for a more authentic experience.

Peppermint Hot Chocolate

Hot chocolate is a childhood classic. This grownup version is just as tasty (if not more). Add some Kahlua or peppermint schnapps to really amp up your hot chocolate.

Yields: 6 servings – Preparation Time: 5 minutes – Cooking Time: 3 hours

Nutrition facts per serving: calories 355, total fat 33 g, carbs 19 g, protein 4 g, sodium 23 mg

Ingredients
4 cups coconut milk
⅓ cup cocoa powder
⅓ cup maple syrup (or agave nectar)
½ teaspoon peppermint extract

Optional:
Coconut whipped cream
Crushed candy cane

Preparation
1. Mix all ingredients together, then cook covered on low for 3 hours or on high for 1½ hours.
2. Serve immediately or leave on warm setting.

Soups

Ginger Carrot Soup

This soup is warm and delicious—plus, ginger is a natural antibiotic perfect for when you're sick. This soup is sure to cure what ails you!

Yields: 4 servings – Preparation Time: 8 hours – Cooking Time: 4 hours

Nutrition facts per serving: calories 220, total fat 12 g, carbs 21 g, protein 3 g, sodium 282 mg

Ingredients
6 carrots, peeled and chopped
1 sweet potato, peeled and chopped
1 onion, diced
4 cups vegetable broth
1 can coconut milk, unsweetened, full fat

1½ teaspoons curry powder
1 tablespoon fresh ginger, peeled and minced
1 clove garlic, minced

Preparation

1. Combine all ingredients in the slow cooker. Cook on low for at least 7 hours, or on high for 3 hours.
2. Use an immersion blender to blend the soup, or pour all ingredients into a traditional blender.
3. Serve warm.

Split Pea Soup

Split pea soup makes for a nutritious addition to any meal. Pair with a salad for the healthiest lunch in town.

Yields: 4 servings – Preparation Time: 15 minutes – Cooking Time: 4 hours

Nutrition facts per serving: calories 272, total fat 1 g, carbs 75 g, protein 25 g, sodium 297 mg

Ingredients
1 pound split peas, rinsed and dried
6 cups vegetable broth
2 carrots, peeled and diced
2 celery stalks, diced
3 cloves garlic, minced
1 onion, diced
1 bay leaf
1 teaspoon cumin
1 teaspoon sage
1 teaspoon thyme
Salt and pepper (to taste)

Preparation

1. Add all ingredients to the slow cooker. Cook covered on low for at least 4 hours.
2. Serve as is, or blend until smooth with an immersion blender.

Corn Chowder

Corn chowder is so creamy and decadent. No reason for vegans to miss out on the flavors of New England.

Yields: 4 servings – Preparation Time: 10 minutes – Cooking Time: 6 hours

Nutrition facts per serving: calories 265, total fat 13 g, carbs 33 g, protein 5 g, sodium 147 mg

Ingredients
2 medium potatoes, washed and chopped
1 onion, chopped
3 cups corn kernels (fresh is better)
2 cloves garlic, minced
1 8-ounce can coconut milk, full fat
4 cups vegetable broth
2 tablespoons vegan butter
1 teaspoon smoked paprika
½ teaspoon red pepper flakes
1 bay leaf
Salt and pepper

<u>Optional:</u>
1 tablespoon cognac

Preparation
1. Add all ingredients to the slow cooker, omitting half of the corn and butter. Cook on low for at least 6 hours, or half that time on high.
2. Use an immersion blender to create a creamy consistency. Add the butter and the rest of the corn and allow to cook for another 10-15 minutes, or until warmed through.
3. Serve warm. Add hot sauce to taste.

Loaded Baked Potato Soup

Think soup can't be filling? You'll change your tune after you try this vegan comfort food.

Yields: 4 servings – Preparation Time: 10 minutes – Cooking Time: 8 hours

*Nutrition facts per serving: calories 259, total fat 12 g,
carbs 33 g, protein 6 g, sodium 152 mg*

Ingredients
4–6 medium potatoes
1 onion, chopped
5 cups vegetable broth
½ cup white beans, canned, rinsed
2–3 cloves garlic, minced
2 tablespoons vegan butter
1 cup vegan milk
Salt and pepper

<u>Optional Toppings:</u>
Vegan cheddar
Vegan sour cream
Tempeh bacon
Chives
Hot sauce
Fried onions

Preparation

1. Add all soup ingredients, except for the vegan milk and white beans, to the slow cooker. Cook covered on low for 8 hours or until potatoes are very tender. If you're in a hurry, you can cook on high for 4 hours.
2. Pour in the non-dairy milk and white beans. Heat until warm and creamy, about 10-15 minutes more.
3. Use the immersion blender to create a smooth consistency.
4. Serve with desired toppings.

Homey Tomato Soup

Nothing like Mom's tomato soup and grilled cheese. This one has all the flavor while remaining cruelty free.

Yields: 4 servings – Preparation Time: 10 minutes – Cooking Time: 6 hours

Nutrition facts per serving: calories 284, total fat 9 g, carbs 42 g, protein 10 g, sodium 596 mg

Ingredients
28 ounces diced tomatoes, canned, drained and rinsed
4 cups vegetable stock
½ cup cashews, soaked
½ cup sundried tomatoes
4 cloves garlic, minced
8 ounces tomato paste
1 red pepper, chopped
1 teaspoon oregano
1 teaspoon basil
½ teaspoon red pepper flakes
Salt and pepper

Optional:
Vegan Parmesan
Fresh basil

Preparation

1. Soak the cashews in water as you prep and cook.
2. Add all ingredients, aside from the cashews, to the slow cooker. Cook covered on low for 6 hours.
3. Add the soaked cashews and blend with an immersion blender.
4. Serve warm with desired toppings.

Turmeric Apple Soup

Turmeric has been shown to have countless health benefits. This soup is a delicious way to eat turmeric, and it's also a great way to utilize those fall harvest apples!

Yields: 6 servings – Preparation Time: 10 minutes – Cooking Time: 6 hours

*Nutrition facts per serving: calories 255, total fat 13 g,
carbs 32 g, protein 4 g, sodium 270 mg*

Ingredients
3 medium apples, chopped
2 large sweet potatoes, peeled and chopped
2 cloves garlic
1 onion, diced
1 inch fresh ginger, peeled and minced
½ cup cashews, soaked
4 cups vegetable broth
1 teaspoon turmeric
Salt and pepper

Preparation

1. Add all ingredients, besides the cashews, to the slow cooker. Cook on low for 6 hours or until vegetables are very tender. Soak the cashews while cooking.
2. When the vegetables are ready, add the cashews, then blend until smooth. Season with salt and pepper and serve warm.

Main Courses

Butternut Squash Alfredo

Buttery, complex, and creamy, this pasta elevates comfort food to the realm of gourmet.

Yields: 4 servings – Preparation Time: 10 minutes – Cooking Time: 8½ hours

Nutrition facts per serving: calories 517, total fat 4 g, carbs 104 g, protein 18 g, sodium 127 mg

Ingredients
½ large butternut squash, peeled and cubed
1 onion
¼ cup white wine, dry
2 tablespoons vegan butter
1 teaspoon thyme
3 cups vegetable broth

2 cups dry pasta
Salt and pepper

Optional:
Vegan Parmesan

Preparation
1. Add the butternut squash, wine, garlic, onion, and butter to the slow cooker. Cook on low for 8 hours, stirring and adding vegetable broth as needed.
2. Add the thyme, remaining vegetable broth, and pasta. Cook on high until pasta is tender. This could take up to 30 minutes or more depending on the type of pasta used.

Protein-Packed Chili

For the days when you need a hearty, protein-packed meal, look no further than this chili. Also perfect for camping trips!

Yields: 4 servings – Preparation Time: 15 minutes – Cooking Time: 8 hours

Nutrition facts per serving: calories 263, total fat 2 g, carbs 51 g, protein 16 g, sodium 702 mg

Ingredients

1 15-ounce can kidney beans, drained and rinsed
1 can black beans, drained and rinsed
1 can chili beans
10 tomatoes, diced
2 onions, diced
2 bell peppers, any color, diced
2 tablespoons chili powder
2 teaspoons cumin
1 teaspoon garlic powder
1 cup dark beer
½ teaspoon cayenne powder
Salt and pepper

Optional toppings:
Jalapeno peppers
Vegan cheddar
Avocado
Vegan sour cream

Preparation

1. Add all ingredients to the crock pot and cook on low for 8 hours.
2. Serve warm with desired toppings.

Coconut Curry

Not only is curry delicious, studies show it may be effective in cancer prevention! All the more reason to add this flavor-filled curry into your life.

Yields: 4 servings – Preparation Time: 10 minutes – Cooking Time: 8½ hours

Nutrition facts per serving: calories 348, total fat 17 g, carbs 41 g, protein 14 g, sodium 632 mg

Ingredients
1 can coconut milk, full fat
2 tablespoons tahini
1 sweet potato, peeled and cubed (or 1 cup butternut squash)
1 16-ounce can chickpeas, drained and rinsed
1 small head cauliflower, cut into florets
4 cloves garlic, minced
1 inch ginger, peeled and shredded
2 tablespoons curry powder
2 tablespoons soy sauce

Preparation
1. Add all ingredients to the slow cooker and cook on high for up to 4 hours, until all vegetables are tender.
2. Serve warm with naan or over quinoa.

Masala Lentils

Lentils are filled with iron and protein, so they're a staple every vegan should include in their diet. This Indian inspired version will definitely add some spice to your week.

Yields: 6 servings – Preparation Time: 15 minutes – Cooking Time: 6 hours

Nutrition facts per serving: calories 274, total fat 10 g, carbs 32 g, protein 15 g, sodium 128 mg

Ingredients
2 cups brown lentils, dry
4 cups vegetable broth
1 cup coconut milk, full fat
1 tablespoon vegan butter
4 cloves garlic, minced
1 inch ginger, peeled and shredded
1 tablespoon garam masala
1 teaspoon maple syrup
2 tomatoes, diced

Preparation
1. Add all ingredients to the slow cooker and cook on high for 4 hours or on low for up to 6 hours.
2. Serve warm with naan or over grain.

Tomato Basil Risotto

Risotto is a delicious comfort food. Naturally creamy Arborio rice is a vegan secret ingredient.

Yields: 6 servings – Preparation Time: 15 minutes – Cooking Time: 2 hours

Nutrition facts per serving: calories 471, total fat 3 g, carbs 92 g, protein 9 g, sodium 93 mg

Ingredients
1 cup Arborio rice
1 cup white wine, dry
3 cups vegetable broth
¼ cup fresh basil
3 cloves garlic
3 tomatoes, medium, diced
1 tablespoon vegan butter
Salt and pepper

Vegan Parmesan

Preparation
1. Add all ingredients, except for the basil and butter, to the slow cooker.
2. Cook on high for 2 hours, or until all liquid has absorbed and rice is tender. Add more liquid as needed.
3. When the rice has finished cooking, add the butter and basil. Mix together and serve warm.

Stuffed Acorn Squash

Acorn squash captures the flavors of fall. Take full advantage of the season by serving up this squash in one of its many forms.

Yields: 2 servings – Preparation Time: 15 minutes – Cooking Time: 8 hours

Nutrition facts per serving: calories 532, total fat 21 g, carbs 75 g, protein 13 g, sodium 25 mg

Ingredients

1 acorn squash, cut in half and seeded
1 cup wild rice, cooked
1 cup brown rice, cooked
1 clove garlic, minced
¼ cup white wine
1 tablespoon olive oil
½ cup walnuts, chopped
½ cup pomegranate seeds
2 teaspoons sage, dried
Salt and pepper

Preparation

1. In a large bowl, combine all ingredients, aside from the squash and pomegranate seeds.
2. Stuff the inside of the squash with the mixture.
3. Fill the bottom of the slow cooker with about a half inch of water. Place the squash in the water and slow cook covered and on low for 8 hours. Serve topped with pomegranate seeds.

Vegan Lo-Mein

This Chinese inspired dish is healthy, easy to make, and a great way to shake up your weekly meal prep. The veggies listed are just a recommendation; feel free to use whatever you have available.

Yields: 2 servings – Preparation Time: 10 minutes – Cooking Time: 1 hour

Nutrition facts per serving: calories 461, total fat 2 g, carbs 93 g, protein 17 g, sodium 713 mg

Ingredients
3 tablespoons hoisin sauce
2½ tablespoons soy sauce (low sodium preferred)
1 tablespoon maple syrup
1 tablespoon rice vinegar (optional)
3 garlic cloves, minced
1½ tablespoons fresh ginger, peeled and shredded
2 bell peppers
1 carrot, peeled and chopped
½ cup mushrooms

½ cup snow peas
½ cup vegetable broth
3 cups whole wheat linguine noodles, cooked (or rice noodles)

Optional Toppings:
Fried tofu
Edamame

Preparation
1. Add all vegetables, sauces, and broth to the slow cooker. Cook on high for 1 hour, or until vegetables are tender.
2. Add cooked noodles and stir together until warm.

Mushroom Bourguignon

Mushrooms are a nutritional powerhouse and a perfect replacement for beef in vegan recipes. This vegan interpretation of the French gourmet dish is sure to impress.

Yields: 2 servings – Preparation Time: 15 minutes – Cooking Time: 8 hours

Nutrition facts per serving: calories 363, total fat 12 g, carbs 37 g, protein 12 g, sodium 636 mg

Ingredients
1 pound mushrooms, variety, raw (about 4–6 cups)
5 cloves garlic
1 cup red wine, dry
2 tablespoons vegan butter
1 onion, diced
3 tablespoons tomato paste
1 cup mushroom broth
2 carrots, peeled and chopped

1–2 tablespoons flour (optional)
1 teaspoon thyme
Salt and pepper

Preparation

1. Add all ingredients to the slow cooker. Cook covered on low for 5–8 hours. Stir occasionally and add liquid as needed.
2. Once the mushrooms have created a thick sauce, serve over egg noodles or mashed potatoes.

Vegan Stroganoff

Stroganoff is originally an Eastern European dish, but now there are dozens of different varieties. Try this vegan version for a taste of the Old Country.

Yields: 2 servings – Preparation Time: 15 minutes – Cooking Time: 5 hours

Nutrition facts per serving: calories 379, total fat 16 g, carbs 38 g, protein 16 g, sodium 563 mg

Ingredients
1 10-ounce package "beefless" beef tips
1 onion, diced
3 cloves garlic, minced
2 carrots, peeled and chopped
¼ -½ cup vegan sour cream
1 tablespoon cognac
1 tablespoon vegan butter
1 teaspoon paprika

2 cups vegetable broth

2 tablespoons tomato paste (or ketchup)

1 tablespoon vegan Worcestershire sauce (optional)

1 16-ounce package egg-free egg noodles

Preparation

1. Add all ingredients, EXCEPT the egg noodles, to the slow cooker and stir well. Cook on low for 5 hours.
2. 15-20 minutes before serving, cook egg noodles according to instructions.
3. Serve over cooked egg noodles.

Truffle Oil Mac & Cheese

Who says mac & cheese is for kids? Upgrade your mac & cheese with vegan replacements and truffle oil.

Yields: 4 servings – Preparation Time: 10 minutes – Cooking Time: 6 hours

Nutrition facts per serving: calories 400, total fat 19 g, carbs 46 g, protein 18 g, sodium 116 mg

Ingredients
6 ounces dry pasta (elbow macaroni preferred)
1 cup cashews, soaked for at least 6 hours
¼ cup nutritional yeast
1 cup vegan milk, unsweetened
¼ cup white wine (optional)
1 tablespoon truffle oil
2 cups water
Salt and pepper

Preparation

1. In a blender, blend together the cashews, milk, and nutritional yeast until very smooth.
2. Add the cashew mixture to the slow cooker with the rest of the ingredients, omitting the truffle oil, and cook on slow for up to 6 hours until the pasta is cooked. Stir in truffle oil and serve warm.

Veggie Fajitas

Did you know that one red pepper has more vitamin C than a lemon? Next time you're feeling under the weather, try these easy, healthy fajitas.

Yields: 4 servings – Preparation Time: 10 minutes – Cooking Time: 4 hours

Nutrition facts per serving: calories 201, total fat 4 g, carbs 36 g, protein 6 g, sodium 810 mg

Ingredients
4 flour tortillas
4 bell peppers, any color, sliced
2 onions, sliced
½ lime, juiced
2 teaspoons fajita seasoning
2 cloves garlic, minced
1 tablespoon vegetable oil

<u>Optional toppings:</u>
Guacamole
Salsa
Corn, fresh
Vegan cheddar

Preparation

1. Add veggies to the slow cooker, toss in oil and seasoning. Cook on low for up to 4 hours.
2. Serve on flour tortillas with chosen toppings.

Hearty Meatloaf

Meatloaf is a hearty American classic you don't have to forget about when you go vegan.

Yields: 4 servings – Preparation Time: 10 minutes – Cooking Time: 4–6 hours

Nutrition facts per serving: calories 343, total fat 11 g, carbs 50 g, protein 14 g, sodium 266 mg

Ingredients
½ cup rolled oats
½ cup cashews, chopped
¼ cup ketchup
1 onion, diced
1 cup carrots, shredded
2 garlic cloves, minced
1½ cups lentils, cooked
1 teaspoon salt
1 teaspoon thyme
2 flax eggs

Preparation

1. Mix everything together in a bowl.
2. Line the slow cooker and fill with the mixture. Shape.
   Cook on low for 6–8 hours or on high for 4–5 hours.
3. Serve warm with bread, green beans, or mashed
   potatoes.

Cottage Pie

This protein-filled comfort food is sure to delight everybody. Hey, where did the meat go?

Yields: 4 servings – Preparation Time: 10 minutes – Cooking Time: 4–6 hours

Nutrition facts per serving: calories 374, total fat 3 g, carbs 82 g, protein 32 g, sodium 142 mg

Ingredients
3 cups mashed potatoes
1 cup lentils, dry
3 cups vegetable broth
½ cup red wine, dry
2 carrots, peeled and chopped
1 onion, diced
2 cloves garlic, minced

½ cup cauliflower
1 tablespoon tomato paste
1 teaspoon thyme

Preparation

1. Add lentils, veggies, broth, wine, and seasoning to the slow cooker and cook covered on high for 1 hour.
2. Spoon mashed potatoes over the lentils and cook on low for up to 3 hours.
3. Serve warm. Finish with vegan cheddar if desired.

Garlic Spaghetti Squash

This spaghetti squash is a surefire way to please low-carb and gluten-free friends. This recipe really couldn't be any easier to make.

Yields: 2 servings – Preparation Time: 10 minutes – Cooking Time: 4–6 hours

Nutrition facts per serving: calories 274, total fat 25 g, carbs 25 g, protein 11 g, sodium 733 mg

Ingredients
1 spaghetti squash
½ cup cashews, unsalted
2 tablespoons nutritional yeast
1 teaspoon garlic powder
¼ teaspoon salt
1 tablespoon vegan butter (or olive oil)

Preparation

1. Prick the outside of the spaghetti squash a few times. Fill the bottom of the slow cooker with about an inch of water.
2. Place the whole squash inside and cook for 6 hours on low.
3. While the squash is cooking, add the cashews, salt, nutritional yeast, and garlic powder to the food processor to make a garlic-flavored Parmesan replacement.
4. Slice the squash in half, scoop out the seeds, and shred the insides with a fork.
5. Serve topped with vegan butter and your vegan Parmesan.

Loaded Potatoes

These loaded potatoes are actually a different take on nachos!
Packed with flavor and protein.

Yields: 4 servings – Preparation Time: 10 minutes – Cooking Time: 5 hours

*Nutrition facts per serving: calories 442, total fat 17 g,
carbs 70 g, protein 12 g, sodium 596 mg*

Ingredients

4 large potatoes, halved, not peeled
1 cup black beans, cooked
1 cup sweet corn
1 cup vegan cheddar cheese
2 bell peppers, diced
2 tablespoons taco seasoning
2 tablespoons olive oil

Optional toppings:
"Beefless" ground beef
Avocado
Vegan sour cream

Preparation

1. Toss potatoes in olive oil and cook on high for 3 hours, until slightly tender.
2. Fill the center of the potatoes with cheese, beans, corn, peppers, and seasoning. Cook on high for another 2 hours until potatoes are fully cooked and the cheese is melted.
3. Serve with desired toppings.

Vegan Lasagna

Who doesn't love cheesy lasagna? This version is a perfect option for Meatless Mondays.

Yields: 6 servings – Preparation Time: 10 minutes – Cooking Time: 5 hours

Nutrition facts per serving: calories 577, total fat 24 g, carbs 75 g, protein 16 g, sodium 797 mg

Ingredients
1 24-ounce jar tomato sauce
24 ounces vegan ricotta cheese
½ cup vegan Parmesan cheese
1 eggplant, sliced
1 package lasagna noodles
1 tablespoon olive oil

Preparation

1. Coat the bottom of the slow cooker with tomato sauce and olive oil.
2. Create layers by stacking pasta, ricotta, eggplant, and tomato sauce until you have filled the pot. Some people like more pasta, others like less, so this is up to you.
3. Top with vegan Parmesan.
4. Cook covered on high for 3 hours. Allow the lasagna to sit after it is done cooking to absorb remaining moisture.

Butternut Dahl

Creamy dhal? Buttery squash? Butternut squash dhal is a match made in heaven.

Yields: 4 servings – Preparation Time: 10 minutes – Cooking Time: 8 hours

Nutrition facts per serving: calories 385, total fat 19 g, carbs 43 g, protein 14 g, sodium 216 mg

Ingredients

1 cup red lentils, dry

2 cups butternut squash, peeled and cubed

2 cloves garlic, minced

2 tablespoons fresh ginger, peeled and minced

1 tablespoon curry powder

1 tablespoon soy sauce, low sodium

2 cups vegetable broth

1½ cups coconut milk, full fat

Preparation

1. Add all ingredients to the slow cooker and cook covered on low for 8 hours.
2. Serve warm over grain or with naan.

White Bean Orzo

This Mediterranean dish makes for a delightful dinner. Serve leftovers cold the next day for lunch.

Yields: 4 servings – Preparation Time: 10 minutes – Cooking Time: 3 hours

Nutrition facts per serving: calories 495, total fat 7 g, carbs 90 g, protein 20 g, sodium 68 mg

Ingredients
1½ cups orzo pasta, dry
1 cup mushrooms, sliced
½ cup green peas (optional)
3 cups vegetable broth
1 15-ounce can white beans, rinsed and drained
1 onion, diced
2 cloves garlic, minced
2 teaspoons Italian seasoning
2 tablespoons vegan butter
Salt and pepper

Preparation

1. Add all ingredients to the slow cooker, except for the pasta and canned beans. Cook covered on high for 1–2 hours.
2. Add pasta and beans and cook on high for up to 45 minutes, until pasta is tender.

"Butter" Chickpeas

This vegan take on an Indian classic is filled with nutrients that vegans sometimes miss out on.

Yields: 4 servings – Preparation Time: 15 minutes – Cooking Time: 5 hours

Nutrition facts per serving: calories 482, total fat 37 g, carbs 30 g, protein 17 g, sodium 627 mg

Ingredients
1 12-ounce package firm tofu, pressed, cubed
1 15-ounce can chickpeas, drained and rinsed
2 tablespoons vegan butter
1 15-ounce can coconut milk, full fat
1 6-ounce can tomato paste
1 tablespoon fresh ginger, peeled and minced
3 cloves garlic, minced
1 tablespoon curry powder
1 tablespoon garam masala

Preparation
1. Add all ingredients to the slow cooker and cook on low for 5 hours. The sauce should be very thick when it's ready.

Sides

Glazed Brussels Sprouts

Brussels sprouts aren't for everyone, but this recipe might convince some people to reconsider.

Yields: 4 servings – Preparation Time: 0 minutes – Cooking Time: 2 hours

*Nutrition facts per serving: calories 115, total fat 6 g,
carbs 14 g, protein 1 g, sodium 77 mg*

Ingredients
1 pound Brussels sprouts
⅓ cup balsamic vinegar
2 tablespoons maple syrup
2 tablespoons vegan butter
Salt and pepper

<u>Optional toppings:</u>
Vegan Parmesan

Preparation

1. Add Brussels sprouts to the slow cooker with salt, pepper and butter and cook on high for 1–2 hours.
2. Meanwhile, bring the balsamic vinegar and maple syrup to a boil in a saucepan. Reduce to a simmer and simmer for 8 minutes.
3. Serve Brussels sprouts warm, covered in the balsamic glaze.

Baked Sweet Potatoes

This is a versatile and nutrient-dense side dish. Serve it on Thanksgiving or at a BBQ.

Yields: 4 servings – Preparation Time: 0 minutes – Cooking Time: 4 hours

Nutrition facts per serving: calories 105, total fat 0 g, carbs 24 g, protein 2 g, sodium 280 mg

Ingredients

4 sweet potatoes

<u>Optional toppings:</u>
Vegan butter
Cinnamon
Maple syrup
Stuffing
Salt and pepper

Preparation

1. Wrap the sweet potatoes in aluminum foil. Cook on high for 4 hours.
2. Serve warm with desired toppings.

Jamaican Rice and Beans

This taste of the Caribbean is an easy way to add more protein to any meal.

Yields: 6 servings – Preparation Time: 0 minutes – Cooking Time: 8 hours

Nutrition facts per serving: calories 329, total fat 16 g, carbs 46 g, protein 10 g, sodium 95 mg

Ingredients
1 15-ounce can coconut milk, full fat
1 cup white rice, dry
1 cup red beans, dry
3 cups vegetable broth
2 limes
1 onion, diced
3 cloves garlic, minced
1 bay leaf
2 teaspoons creole spice
Salt

Preparation

1. Add all ingredients, except for the limes, to the slow cooker and cook covered on low for 8 hours until beans are tender and all liquid has evaporated.
2. Serve with lime juice.

Maple Glazed Carrots

Maple syrup elevates these carrots to a gourmet side perfect with a vegan roast or holiday meal.

Yields: 4 servings – Preparation Time: 10 minutes – Cooking Time: 3 hours

Nutrition facts per serving: calories 180, total fat 11 g, carbs 20 g, protein 0 g, sodium 137 mg

Ingredients

1 pound carrots, peeled and chopped
¼ cup vegan butter
¼ cup maple syrup
1 tablespoon apple cider vinegar
Salt and pepper

Preparation

1. Combine all ingredients in the slow cooker and cook covered on high for 1 hour.
2. Stir.
3. Cook for an additional 2 hours on low.

Buttery Mushroom Rice

This flavor-filled rice goes great with a vegan roast or grilled veggies.

Yields: 4 servings – Preparation Time: 10 minutes – Cooking Time: 6 hours

*Nutrition facts per serving: calories 297, total fat 10 g,
carbs 43 g, protein 7 g, sodium 241 mg*

Ingredients

½ pound mushrooms, sliced

2 tablespoons vegan butter

1 onion, diced

3 cloves garlic

1 teaspoon thyme

1 cup rice, white

2 cups vegetable broth

½ cup vegan Parmesan

Preparation

1. Add all ingredients to the slow cooker and cook covered on low for 6 hours or on high for half that time.

Snack Mix

A perfect and easy treat you can bring to any party or throw in a lunchbox in the morning.

Yields: 10 servings – Preparation Time: 0 minutes – Cooking Time: 2 hours

*Nutrition facts per serving: calories 84, total fat 3 g,
carbs 13 g, protein 2 g, sodium 284 mg*

Ingredients
3 cups cereal of your choice (variety recommended)
1 cup mini pretzels
1 cup bagel chips
2 tablespoons vegan butter

½ teaspoon garlic powder
½ teaspoon onion powder
¼ teaspoon paprika
½ teaspoon salt

Preparation

1. Pour cereal, pretzels, and bagel chips into the slow cooker.
2. In a separate bowl, melt butter and mix together with seasonings. Pour over cereal mixture.
3. Cook on high for 2 hours, uncovered.
4. Eat right away or store in an airtight container.

Stuffed Peppers

You can stuff peppers with just about whatever you have in the pantry, but this recipe is one very tasty combo. Serve this healthy side at a fiesta or picnic.

Yields: 4 servings – Preparation Time: 10 minutes – Cooking Time: 6 hours

*Nutrition facts per serving: calories 200, total fat 9 g,
carbs 25 g, protein 6 g, sodium 260 mg*

Ingredients
4 bell peppers, any color, cored
4 tomatoes, diced
1 onion, diced
1 cup quinoa, cooked
1 cup "beefless" ground beef
1 teaspoon taco seasoning
½ teaspoon paprika

Preparation
1. In a large bowl, combine all ingredients other than the peppers.
2. Stuff each pepper with the mixture. Fill the bottom of the slow cooker with about ¼ to ½ of an inch of water.
3. Cook the peppers on low for 6 hours.

Southern Style Green Beans

This nutrient-dense, protein-filled side goes great with traditional American food and holiday meals. Enjoy it at home or bring to a summer BBQ.

Yields: 4 servings – Preparation Time: 0 minutes – Cooking Time: 3 hours

Nutrition facts per serving: calories 41, total fat 0 g, carbs 7 g, protein 4 g, sodium 67 mg

Ingredients
6 slices tempeh bacon
1 pound fresh green beans
½ onion, diced
½ cup vegetable broth
1 teaspoon thyme
Salt and pepper

Preparation
1. Add all ingredients to the slow cooker and cook covered on high for 3 hours, until green beans are tender.

Cajun Potatoes

Channel the flavors of New Orleans into everyone's favorite carb.

Yields: 4 servings – Preparation Time: 0 minutes – Cooking Time: 3 hours

Nutrition facts per serving: calories 294, total fat 4 g, carbs 45 g, protein 2 g, sodium 365 mg

Ingredients

3 potatoes, cubed or wedged

4 links vegan sausage, sliced

1 cup corn

½ cup vegetable broth

1–2 teaspoons Cajun seasoning

½ teaspoon red pepper flakes

Salt and pepper

Preparation

1. Add all ingredients to the slow cooker. Cook on low for 7 hours, until potatoes are tender.

Desserts

Apple Nachos

These dessert nachos are a brilliant way to trick your kids into eating fruit.

Yields: 4 servings – Preparation Time: 10 minutes – Cooking Time: 3 hours

Nutrition facts per serving: calories 193, total fat 6 g, carbs 34 g, protein 0 g, sodium 65 mg

Ingredients
4 apples, sliced
2 tablespoons vegan butter
1 teaspoon cinnamon
½ teaspoon ginger
2 tablespoons brown sugar

Optional toppings:

Maple syrup

Caramel sauce

Nut butter

Carob chips

Raisins

Vegan marshmallows

Preparation

1. Place ingredients in the slow cooker and cook covered on low for 3 hours, or until apples have reached your desired tenderness.
2. Finish with desired toppings.

Chai Tea Pie

The warm flavors of this pie make a uniquely delicious treat.
Bring it to a holiday party for a real knockout.

Yields: 6 servings – Preparation Time: 0 minutes – Cooking Time: 8 hours

*Nutrition facts per serving: calories 347, total fat 24 g,
carbs 33 g, protein 3 g, sodium 155 mg*

Ingredients
1 15-ounce can coconut milk, full fat
¼-½ cup maple syrup (to taste)
1 tablespoon cinnamon
6 cloves
6 cardamom pods
1 teaspoon ground ginger
2 tablespoons flour
1 pie crust (or 6 mini pie crusts)

Preparation
1. Add the coconut milk and spices to the slow cooker. Cook covered on low for 6 hours, stirring occasionally.
2. Remove the cardamom pods and cloves. Slowly stir in flour until the coconut milk thickens. Add the maple syrup. Cook covered on low for up to 2 more hours, until the milk has thickened once more.
3. Pour the mixture into a pie crust and refrigerate for 45 minutes.

Hot Fudge Cake

Who says vegans can't eat gooey, decadent chocolate cake?
Perfect for a summer picnic.

Yields: 12 servings – Preparation Time: 5 minutes – Cooking Time: 3 hours

*Nutrition facts per serving: calories 349, total fat 13 g,
carbs 57 g, protein 4 g, sodium 90 mg*

Ingredients

2 cups maple syrup

2 flax eggs

2 cups flour

¾ cup cocoa powder

1 cup vegan milk

½ cup vegan butter (or coconut oil)

1 tablespoon baking powder

2 teaspoons vanilla extract

1 cup water (as needed)

Preparation

1. Combine all ingredients in a large bowl, whisking together and adding water as needed.
2. Grease the inside of the slow cooker and pour in the batter.
3. Cook covered on low for 3 hours until cake has set. Use a toothpick to determine when it is ready.

Pumpkin Butter

Pumpkin butter is a fall classic that's high in vitamin A. Eat this on a bagel or use it to make frosting!

Yields: 32 servings – Preparation Time: 0 minutes – Cooking Time: 6 hours

Nutrition facts per serving: calories 25, total fat 0 g, carbs 6 g, protein 0 g, sodium 1 mg

Ingredients
1 15-ounce can pumpkin puree
½ cup maple syrup
¼ cup brown sugar
2 tablespoons pumpkin pie spice mix
½ teaspoon vanilla extract

Preparation

1. Mix all ingredients together in the slow cooker. Cook covered on low for up to 6 hours. Stir regularly to prevent burning and sticking.
2. Store in a jar in the refrigerator for up to 2 weeks.

Rosewater Yogurt

Dessert doesn't have to be filled with sugar and calories. This vegan yogurt will certainly satisfy your sweet tooth nonetheless.

Yields: 4 servings – Preparation Time: 0 minutes – Cooking Time: 10½ hours

*Nutrition facts per serving: calories 80, total fat 3 g,
carbs 11 g, protein 0 g, sodium 115 mg*

Ingredients

4 cups soy or coconut milk

1 tablespoon rosewater

½ cup vegan yogurt or vegan yogurt starter

<u>For serving</u>

Mixed berries

Sweetener

Preparation

1. Place the milk in the slow cooker and cook on low for about 2½ hours. Remove from heat, but leave covered.
2. After the milk sits for 2 hours, stir in the vegan yogurt or starter.
3. Wrap the crock pot in a towel and allow the yogurt to cool for 8 hours in the oven (turned off).
4. The longer the yogurt sits, the sourer and firmer it will become.
5. Stir in rosewater, fruit, and any desired sweetener. Store in the refrigerator.

Poached Pears

When it comes to dessert, pears are seriously underrated. Serve these as a fall favorite or with ice cream at a summer picnic.

Yields: 8 servings – Preparation Time: 10 minutes – Cooking Time: 6 hours

Nutrition facts per serving: calories 147, total fat 3 g, carbs 32 g, protein 0 g, sodium 36 mg

Ingredients
4 pears, halved, cored, and peeled
1 cup brown sugar, unpacked
2 tablespoons vegan butter
1 tablespoon cinnamon
1 teaspoon ground ginger
1 whole star anise

Preparation
1. Mix all ingredients together in the slow cooker.
2. Cook on low, covered, for up to 6 hours, until pears are tender.

Recipe Index

Also by Madison Miller

Here are some of Madison Miller's other cookbooks.

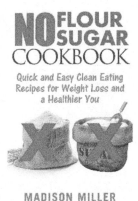

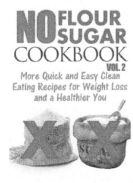

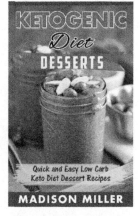

Cooking Conversion Charts

1. Measuring Equivalent Chart

Type	Imperial	Imperial	Metric
Weight	1 dry ounce		28g
	1 pound	16 dry ounces	0.45 kg
Volume	1 teaspoon		5 ml
	1 dessert spoon	2 teaspoons	10 ml
	1 tablespoon	3 teaspoons	15 ml
	1 Australian tablespoon	4 teaspoons	20 ml
	1 fluid ounce	2 tablespoons	30 ml
	1 cup	16 tablespoons	240 ml
	1 cup	8 fluid ounces	240 ml
	1 pint	2 cups	470 ml
	1 quart	2 pints	0.95 l
	1 gallon	4 quarts	3.8 l
Length	1 inch		2.54 cm

*   Numbers are rounded to the closest equivalent

2. Oven Temperature Equivalent Chart

Fahrenheit (°F)	Celsius (°C)	Gas Mark
220	100	
225	110	1/4
250	120	1/2
275	140	1
300	150	2
325	160	3
350	180	4
375	190	5
400	200	6
425	220	7
450	230	8
475	250	9
500	260	

* Celsius (°C) = T (°F)-32] * 5/9

** Fahrenheit (°F) = T (°C) * 9/5 + 32

*** Numbers are rounded to the closest equivalent

Made in the USA
Monee, IL
14 November 2024

70121696R00066